C000175345

Inspirational Quotes Copywork

Practice Cursive Handwriting
with Inspirational Quotes from Great Leaders

Classic Copywork Vol. 2

ISBN: 0692286497
ISBN-13: 978-0692286494

Table of Contents

Abraham Lincoln: Reading

A capacity, and a taste, for reading, gives access to whatever has already been discovered by others. It is the key, or one of the keys, to the already solved problems. And not only so. It gives a relish, and facility, for successfully pursuing the yet unsolved ones.

Abraham Lincoln,
16th President of the United States

A capacity, and a taste, for reading,

gives access to whatever has already been

discovered by others. It is the key,

or one of the keys, to the already solved

problems. And not only so. It gives a

relish, and facility, for successfully

pursuing the yet unsolved ones.

Abraham Lincoln,

16th President of the United States

Thomas Jefferson: Liberty

I would rather be exposed to the inconveniences attending too much liberty than those attending too small a degree of it.

Thomas Jefferson,
3rd President of the United States

I would rather be exposed to the

inconveniences attending too much

liberty than those attending too

small a degree of it.

Thomas Jefferson,

3rd President of the United States

Lao Tzu: Usefulness

The usefulness of a pot comes from its emptiness.

> *Lao Tzu,*
> *Chinese Philosopher and Poet,*
> *Founder of Taoism*

The usefulness of a pot

comes from. its emptiness.

Lao Tzu,

Chinese Philosopher and Poet,

Founder of Taoism

Thomas Edison: Seeming to Do is Not Doing

Being busy does not always mean real work. The object of all work is production or accomplishment, and to either of these ends there must be forethought, system, planning, intelligence, and honest purpose, as well as perspiration. Seeming to do is not doing.

Thomas Edison,
American Inventor and Businessman

Being busy does not always mean real work.

The object of all work is production or

accomplishment, and to either of these ends

there must be forethought, system, planning,

intelligence, and honest purpose, as well as

perspiration. Seeming to do is not doing.

Thomas Edison,

American Inventor and Businessman

Sun Tzu: Victory

If you know the enemy and know yourself,
you need not fear the result of a hundred battles.
If you know yourself but not the enemy,
for every victory gained you will also suffer a defeat.
If you know neither the enemy nor yourself,
you will succumb in every battle.

Sun Tzu,
Chinese General and Philosopher

If you know the enemy and know yourself,

you need not fear the result of a hundred battles.

If you know yourself but not the enemy,

for every victory gained you will also suffer a defeat.

If you know neither the enemy nor yourself,

you will succumb in every battle.

Sun Tzu,

Chinese General and Philosopher

Martin Luther King Jr.: I have a Dream

I have a dream that one day this nation will rise up and live out the true meaning of its creed:

"We hold these truths to be self-evident, that all men are created equal."

I have a dream that my four little children will one day live in a nation where they will not be judged by the color of their skin but by the content of their character.

> *Martin Luther King, Jr.,*
> *Civil Rights Activist and Leader*

I have a dream that one day this nation will rise up

and live out the true meaning of its creed:

"We hold these truths to be self-evident,

that all men are created equal."

I have a dream that my four little children

will one day live in a nation where they will

not be judged by the color of their skin but by

the content of their character.

Martin Luther King, Jr.

Civil Rights Activist and Leader

Ronald Reagan: The American Dream

The American dream is not that every man must be level with every other man. The American dream is that every man must be free to become whatever God intends he should become.

Ronald Reagan,
40th President of the United States

The American dream is not that every man must

be level with every other man. The American dream

is that every man must be free to become

whatever God intends he should become.

Ronald Reagan,

40th President of the United States

Calvin Coolidge: Persistence

Nothing in this world can take the place of persistence.
Talent will not; nothing is more common then unsuccessful men with talent.
Genius will not; unrewarded genius is almost a proverb.
Education will not; the world is full of educated derelicts.
Persistence and determination alone are omnipotent.

Calvin Coolidge,
30th President of the United States

Nothing in this world can take the place of

persistence. Talent will not;

nothing is more common then unsuccessful

men with talent. Genius will not;

unrewarded genius is almost a proverb.

Education will not; the world is full of

educated derelicts. Persistence and

determination alone are omnipotent.

Calvin Coolidge,

30th President of the United States

Dalai Lama: Religion

The very purpose of religion is to control yourself, not to criticize others. Rather, we must criticize ourselves. How much am I doing about my anger? About my attachment, about my hatred, about my pride, my jealousy? These are the things that we must check in daily life.

Dalai Lama,
Tibetan Buddhist Leader

The very purpose of religion is to control yourself,

not to criticize others. Rather, we

must criticize ourselves. How much am I

doing about my anger? About my

attachment, about my hatred, about my

pride, my jealousy? These are the

things that we must check in daily life.

the Dalai Lama,

Tibetan Buddhist Leader

Vince Lombardi: Commitment to Excellence

Most important of all, to be successful in life demands that a man make a personal commitment to excellence and to victory, even though the ultimate victory can never be completely won. Yet that victory must be pursued and wooed with every fiber of our body, with every bit of our might and all of our effort. And each week, there is a new encounter; each day, there is a new challenge.

Vince Lombardi,
American Football Coach

Most important of all, to be successful in life

demands that a man make a personal commitment

to excellence and to victory, even though the

ultimate victory can never be completely won.

Yet that victory must be pursued and wooed with

every fiber of our body, with every bit of our might

and all of our effort. And each week, there is a

new encounter; each day, there is a new challenge.

Vince Lombardi,

American Football Coach

Nelson Mandela: Hate and Love

No one is born hating another person because of the colour of his skin, or his background, or his religion. People must learn to hate, and if they can learn to hate, they can be taught to love, for love comes more naturally to the human heart than its opposite.

Nelson Mandela,
Former President of South Africa

No one is born hating another person because

of the colour of his skin, or his background,

or his religion. People must learn to hate,

and if they can learn to hate, they can be

taught to love, for love comes more naturally

to the human heart than its opposite.

Nelson Mandela,

Former President of South Africa

John Fitzgerald Kennedy: Challenge

*We choose to go to the moon in this decade and do the other
things, not because they are easy, but because they are hard,
because that goal will serve to organize and measure the best
of our energies and skills, because that challenge is one that
we are willing to accept, one we are unwilling to postpone,
and one which we intend to win.*

*John Fitzgerald Kennedy ("JFK"),
35th President of the United States*

We choose to go to the moon in this decade and,

do the other things not because they are easy,

but because they are hard, because that goal

will serve to measure and organize the best

of our energies and skills, because that

challenge is one that we are willing to

accept, one we are unwilling to postpone,

and one which we intend to win.

John Fitzgerald Kennedy,

35th President of the United States

Margaret Mead: Change the World

Never doubt that a small group of thoughtful,
committed citizens can change the world:
indeed, it's the only thing that ever has.

Margaret Mead,
American Anthropologist

Never doubt that a small group of thoughtful,

committed citizens can change the world:

indeed it's the only thing that ever has.

Margaret Mead,

American Anthropologist

Ray Bradbury: Educating Yourself

I spent three days a week for ten years educating myself in the public library, and it's better than college. People should educate themselves - you can get a complete education for no money. At the end of ten years, I had read every book in the library and I'd written a thousand stories.

Ray Bradbury,
American Novelist,
Essayist, and Playwright

I spent three days a week for ten years educating

myself in the public library, and it's better

than college. People should educate themselves - you

can get a complete education for no money.

At the end of ten years, I had read every book in

the library and I'd written a thousand stories.

Ray Bradbury, American Novelist,

Essayist, and Playwright

Helen Keller: Optimism

Every optimist moves along with progress and hastens it, while every pessimist would keep the world at a standstill. The consequence of pessimism in the life of a nation is the same as in the life of the individual. Pessimism kills the instinct that urges people to struggle against poverty, ignorance, and crime, and dries up all the fountains of joy in the world. Optimism is the faith that leads to achievement; nothing can be done without hope.

> *Helen Keller,*
> *Blind and Deaf Writer and Social Activist*

Every optimist moves along with progress and
hastens it, while every pessimist would keep the
world at a standstill. The consequence of
pessimism in the life of a nation is the same as
in the life of the individual. Pessimism kills
the instinct that urges people to struggle against
poverty, ignorance, and crime, and dries up
all the fountains of joy in the world. Optimism is
the faith that leads to achievement; nothing can
be done without hope.

Helen Keller,

Blind and Deaf Writer and Social Activist

Alvin Toffler: Many Skills

Society needs people who take care of the elderly and who know how to be compassionate and honest. Society needs people who work in hospitals. Society needs all kinds of skills that are not just cognitive; they're emotional, they're affectional. You can't run the society on data and computers alone.

Alvin Toffler
American Writer and Futurist

Society needs people who take care of the

elderly and who know how to be compassionate

and honest. Society needs people who work in

hospitals. Society needs all kinds of skills that

are not just cognitive; they're emotional, they're

affectional. You can't run the society on data

and computers alone.

Alvin Toffler,

American Writer and Futurist

Mother Teresa: Do Good Anyway

People are often unreasonable and self-centered
Forgive them anyway
If you are kind, people may accuse you of ulterior motives
Be kind anyway
If you are honest, people may cheat you
Be honest anyway
If you find happiness, people may be jealous
Be happy anyway
The good you do today may be forgotten tomorrow
Do good anyway
Give the world the best you have and it may never be enough
Give your best anyway

Mother Teresa,
Catholic Religious Leader

People are often unreasonable and self-centered

Forgive them anyway

If you are kind, people may accuse you of ulterior

motives; Be kind anyway. If you are honest,

people may cheat you; Be honest anyway

If you find happiness, people may be jealous

Be happy anyway

The good you do today may be forgotten tomorrow

Do good anyway

Give the world the best you have and it may never be

enough; Give your best anyway

Mother Teresa, Catholic Religious Leader

Henry Ford: Collected Wisdom

Vision without execution is just hallucination.

Quality means doing it right when no one is looking.

The only real mistake is the one from which we learn nothing.

It has been my observation that most people get ahead during the time that others waste.

Don't find fault, find a remedy; anyone can complain.

You can't build a reputation on what you are going to do.

Henry Ford,
American Industrialist,
Founder of the Ford Motor Company

Vision without execution is just hallucination.

Quality means doing it right when no one is looking.

The only real mistake is the one from which we

learn nothing.

It has been my observation that most people get ahead

during the time that others waste.

Don't find fault, find a remedy; anyone

can complain.

You can't build a reputation on what you are

going to do.

Henry Ford, American Industrialist

and Founder of the Ford Motor Company

Friedrich Koenig: Happiness

We tend to forget that happiness doesn't come as a result of getting something we don't have, but rather of recognizing and appreciating what we do have.

Friedrich Koenig,
German Inventor

We tend to forget that happiness doesn't come

as a result of getting something we don't have,

but rather of recognizing and appreciating

what we do have.

Friedrich Koenig,

German Inventor

Maya Angelou: Courage

One is not necessarily born with courage, but one is born with potential. Without courage, we cannot practice any other virtue with consistency. We can't be kind, true, merciful, generous, or honest.

Maya Angelou,
Author and Poet

One is not necessarily born with courage,

but one is born with potential.

Without courage, we cannot practice any

other virtue with consistency.

We can't be kind, true, merciful, generous, or honest.

Maya Angelou,

Author and Poet

Indira Gandhi: Work

My grandfather once told me that there were two kinds of people: those who do the work and those who take the credit. He told me to try to be in the first group; there was much less competition.

Indira Gandhi,
Former Prime Minister of India

My grandfather once told me that there were

two kinds of people: those who do the

work and those who take the credit.

He told me to try to be in the first group;

there was much less competition.

Indira Gandhi,

Former Prime Minister of India

Will Durant: Excellence

Excellence is an art won by training and habituation. We do not act rightly because we have virtue or excellence, but rather we have these because we have acted rightly. We are what we repeatedly do. Excellence, then, is not an act but a habit.

Will Durant,
American Historian and Philosopher

Excellence is an art won by training and

habituation. We don't act rightly because we

have virtue or excellence, but rather we have

these because we have acted rightly. We are

what we repeatedly do. Excellence, then, is

not an act but a habit.

Will Durant,

American Historian and Philosopher

Plato: Compulsion

Bodily exercise, when compulsory, does no harm to the body; but knowledge which is acquired under compulsion obtains no hold on the mind.

Plato,
Classical Greek Philosopher

Bodily exercise, when compulsory,

does no harm to the body,

but knowledge which is acquired under compulsion

obtains no hold on the mind.

Plato,

Classical Greek Philosopher

Ayn Rand: Vision

Throughout the centuries there were men who took first steps down new roads armed with nothing but their own vision. The great creators – the thinkers, the artists, the scientists, the inventors – stood alone against the men of their time. Every great new thought was opposed; every great new invention was denounced. But those of unborrowed vision went ahead. They fought, they suffered, and they paid. But they won.

Ayn Rand,
American Novelist and Philosopher

Throughout the centuries there were men who

took first steps down new roads armed with

nothing but their own vision.

The great creators — the thinkers, the artists, the

scientists, the inventors — stood alone against

the men of their time. Every great new thought

was opposed; every great new invention was

denounced. But those of unborrowed vision

went ahead. They fought, they suffered, and

they paid. But they won.

Ayn Rand,

American Novelist and Philosopher

Confucius: Learning

He who learns but does not think, is lost!
He who thinks but does not learn is in great danger.

I hear and I forget
I see and I remember
I do and I understand

> *Confucius,*
> *Ancient Chinese Philosopher*

He who learns but does not think, is lost!

He who thinks but does not learn is in great danger.

I hear and I forget

I see and I remember

I do and I understand

Confucius,

Ancient Chinese Philosopher

Black Elk: Little Children

Grown men may learn from very little children, for the hearts of very little children are pure, and therefore the Great Spirit may show to them many things which older people miss.

Black Elk,
Native American Indian Medicine Man

Grown men may learn from very little children,

for the hearts of very little children are pure,

and therefore The Great Spirit may show to them

many things which older people miss.

Black Elk,

Native American Indian Medicine Man

Marie Curie: Science

A scientist in his laboratory is not a mere technician: he is also a child confronting natural phenomena that impress him as though they were fairy tales.

Marie Curie,
Pioneering Scientist and Nobel Prize Winner

A scientist in his laboratory is not a mere

technician: he is also a child confronting

natural phenomena that impress him as

though they were fairy tales.

Marie Curie,

Pioneering Scientist and Nobel Prize Winner

T.E. Lawrence: Dreams

All men dream, but not equally. Those who dream by night in the dusty recesses of their minds wake in the day to find that it was vanity; but the dreamers of the day are dangerous men, for they may act their dreams with open eyes, and make it possible.

> *T.E. Lawrence,*
> *"Lawrence of Arabia"*
> *British Military Leader*

All men dream, but not equally.

Those who dream by night in the dusty recesses of their

minds wake in the day to find that it was vanity;

but the dreamers of the day are dangerous men,

for they may act their dreams with open eyes,

and make it possible.

T.E. Lawrence, "Lawrence of Arabia"

British Military Leader

Mary Ann Evans: Courage

Any coward can fight a battle when he's sure of winning;
but give me the man who has pluck to fight when he's sure of
losing. There are many victories worse than a defeat.

> *Mary Ann Evans,*
> *English Novelist,*
> *Pen Name: George Eliot*

Any coward can fight a battle when he's sure of

winning; but give me the man who

has pluck to fight when he's sure of losing. There

are many victories worse than a defeat.

Mary Ann Evans, English Novelist,

Pen Name: George Eliot

Leonardo da Vinci: Nature

Nature is a source of truth. Experience does not ever err, it is only your judgment that errs in promising itself results which are not caused by your experiments.

Leonardo da Vinci,
Italian Artist and Innovator

Nature is a source of truth. Experience does not

ever err, it is only your judgment that errs

in promising itself results which are not caused

by your experiments.

Leonardo da Vinci,

Italian Artist and Innovator

Albert Einstein: A Man of Value

Try not to become a man of success but rather try to become a man of value.
Look around at how people want to get more out of life than they put in.
A man of value will give more than he receives.

Albert Einstein,
Theoretical Physicist

Try not to become a man of success but

rather try to become a man of value.

Look around at how people want to get more

out of life than they put in.

A man of value will give more than he receives.

Albert Einstein,

Theoretical Physicist

Winston Churchill: Never Surrender

We shall not flag or fail. We shall go on to the end. We shall defend ourselves whatever the cost may be. We shall fight on the beaches, we shall fight on the landing-grounds, we shall fight in the fields and in the streets, we shall fight in the hills. We shall never surrender!

Winston Churchill,
Former Prime Minister of the United Kingdom

We shall not flag or fail. We shall go on to the end.

We shall defend ourselves whatever the cost may be.

We shall fight on the beaches, we shall fight on the

landing-grounds, we shall fight in the fields

and in the streets, we shall fight in the hills.

We shall never surrender!

Winston Churchill,

Former Prime Minister of the United Kingdom

Want More?

Great Literature Cursive Copywork

Practice Handwriting with Excerpts from the Great Books

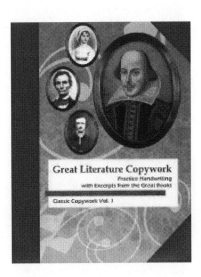

Experience some of the great moments in classic literature and history while improving your cursive handwriting. Copywork is best way to learn basic grammar, spelling, and composition skills, so why practice penmanship with random words and sentences when you could be exploring amazing stories and poems by authors including:

Shakespeare	Abraham Lincoln
Homer	Jane Austen
Aristotle	James Joyce
Robert Frost	Robert Louis Stevenson
Mark Twain	Rudyard Kipling
Edgar Allen Poe	and many more

This copybook includes over 40 passages. Buy online at www.ruthlestina.com.

Printed in Great Britain
by Amazon